101 Games for Self-Esteem

by **Jenny Mosley**
and **Helen Sonnet**

Copyright notice

Acknowledgements

Like you – I have played games all my life! Playing games has always been a way of learning moral values, social skills and how to have fun. They are the pulse and rhythm of everyday life for children and need to be at the heart of the teaching and learning process.

I use games with all the groups I teach, and consequently I learn games from many people. So I would like to thank all of my groups over the years, and some particular individuals that I remember. So here goes:

A big thank you to all the people who have attended my seven day London University SENJIT courses. By the end of each course we are all exchanging brilliant ideas. Particular thanks to Annette Truss for her mobile phone game and Moya Brewer for Rocket launch. Thank you too to all my overseas and home teachers on my MEd modules at Bristol University; I keep learning that all games are universal – they just have different names. Thank you to all the children I meet in playgrounds and circles who are constantly teaching either me or my puppets new games. These young people are far more patient than many parents and teachers (definitely including myself)!

Jenny Mosley

101 Games for Self-Esteem
LL01511
ISBN 1 85503 351 8
© Jenny Mosley and Helen Sonnet
Illustrations by Mark Cripps and Brian Hoskin
All rights reserved
First published 2002

LDA, Duke Street, Wisbech, Cambs, PE13 2AE UK
3195 Wilson Drive NW, Grand Rapids, MI 49544 USA

Contents

Myself, my feelings

Thinking and concentrating

Developing attention skills

Motivating through music

Taking action

Introduction

Self-esteem has long been recognised as an important factor in how people live their lives and relate to others. A positive self-image can lead to effective social skills, healthy relationships and greater confidence and motivation to tackle the challenges of life.

Enhancing self-esteem has been a focus of educationalists in recent years, and playing games is known to be a valuable method to help achieve this. Games are fun and engaging, providing an enjoyable environment in which to teach and encourage children. They are a great way for children to learn how to relate well to others and feel more positive about themselves. Games can also be used to teach valuable skills, such as self-awareness, empathy, cooperation and the confidence to trust.

Some of the games included in this book provide children with the opportunity to experience personal success and enjoy the recognition of their peers. Others focus on promoting interpersonal skills through interaction with others. As children begin to appreciate their similarities and differences, they learn to value the uniqueness and worth of each individual. The interest and enjoyment involved in playing games promotes friendship and trust within a group, helping children to respond to one another in positive ways. Some of the games incorporate role-play, allowing the children to explore and learn, in a safe context, effective and appropriate ways to react in given situations.

The games are organised thematically, so you can decide which are most suitable for a group at a particular time. They can be used at school as a positive way to start and end the day, as part of Circle Time, as warm-ups in PE, as playground games or for special privileges. These games are also ideal for youth clubs and holiday schemes. If you are trying these ideas for the first time, you may decide to start with the games you feel comfortable with and progress to the others when you feel ready. You can use teaching assistants, or other adults, to enable you to divide a large group into smaller and more manageable units.

Many of the games take place in a circle of chairs. A circle provides a democratic framework in which all participants are equal. It is easy to maintain good eye contact with everyone and the quieter members are encouraged to join in. A circle also provides an effective means to organise a game and discuss the outcomes. (A full account of how to conduct Circle Time is given in Quality Circle Time – see Training and resources, page 144.)

Guidelines should be laid down regarding behaviour within the circle, most importantly that no interruptions or negative comments are allowed. The vital message is that everyone's contribution is valid and all participants have an equal right to their say within the circle. Being listened to is an important part of gaining self-respect, and only when they have learnt respect for self can children learn to respect others.

There is a wide variety of games in this book, but the greatest fund of knowledge will probably be the adults and children that you work with. There will be teachers who incorporate games into their lessons, and children who have learnt games at home and holiday schemes. If you ask around you will probably be able to enhance your repertoire of games quite considerably.

So play and enjoy the games in this book. Share together in the fun, humour, discussion, reflection and participation. Observe children as they grow in confidence and self-awareness, with the positive knowledge that these childhood experiences will help shape their adult lives.

Learning to value yourself

The games in this section allow each child a central role, where they have the opportunity to appreciate their own uniqueness, feel they have something valuable to offer and receive positive reinforcement. Each child will be able to proclaim 'This is who I am.' and feel a sense of value.

Coming full circle

This simple inclusive game helps children feel that they belong to a group.

Resources

None

What to do

Taking turns round the circle, each child completes the sentence, 'My name is ... and I am sitting next to ... and ...' The child names the children sitting on either side of them.

Comments

You might like to use a 'talking object' for this game; a small toy or painted egg is ideal. A child speaks only when they are holding the object and they pass it on when their sentence is completed.

You could mix the children up before the activity starts so that they are not sitting next to their best friends. Ask the children to gather in the centre of the circle and quietly sit on the nearest chair at a given signal.

A similar game involves placing an extra chair in the circle. The child sitting to the right of this chair says, 'I would like ... to come and sit next to me because ...' The sentence ends with a positive statement; the child named moves, creating a different empty chair, and the game continues.

Mobile messages

Mobile messages

This game encourages all the children to participate and feel included in the circle. They do not have to think about their contribution and so will not feel intimidated when their turn comes.

Resources

Two toy mobile phones

What to do

Choose two children, or ask for volunteers, to use the phones first. The game proceeds as follows:

> *Whole group:* Ring, ring
>
> *Child A:* Hello *[child B's name]* it's *[child A's name]* calling to wish you a good day.
>
> *Whole group:* Ring, ring
>
> *Child B:* Thank you *[child A's name]*, for calling me. That was a nice thing to say.

The game continues with the phones moving around the group each time.

Comments

You will need to practise this a few times and limit the calls to about six per game. Keep a checklist to make sure everyone gets a turn. To discourage best friends calling each other, you can write the children's names down and put them into a hat. Children then call the person whose name they pick out.

Look what I can do

This game provides a positive focus on each child as they lead the group in performing an action.

Resources

None

What to do

Explore some actions that the children could do, such as hopping, jumping up and down, clapping their hands or stretching up high. Each child in turn chooses an action to perform and says to the group, 'My name is ... and I can ...' The child demonstrates the action and then says, 'Will you all join in with me?' The other children then copy the action. Another child chooses a different action and the game proceeds.

Comments

This is quite a long game so you may want to play it over several sessions. A variation is to play some lively music and call out the children's names in turn. When a child's name is called they perform an action in time to the music for the other children to copy.

Animal antics

This game provides an enjoyable way for children to think about their personal qualities.

Resources

None

What to do

The children choose an animal that they think has qualities similar to their own. Half the group remains seated while the other half moves around in the centre of the circle, pretending to be their animal. The seated children can get up and tap an animal on the shoulder to guess its identity. If the guess is correct, the animal sits down. This continues until all the animals are sitting down. The children then swap roles.

Call the children back to their places and play a game of changing seats according to categories; for example, animals that live in trees, animals covered in fur, animals that are predators. Finish the game with the round 'If I were an animal I would be ... because ...'

Comments

As children become more experienced at this game they will be able to consider character traits in greater depth. It may be a good idea to prompt the children with the sort of qualities they could consider; for example, are they timid or bold, are they solitary or sociable, are they very energetic?

Special delivery

This game provides a positive focus for each child in a setting that is fun.

Resources

None

What to do

One child stands in the middle of the circle. The chairs are numbered. The child in the middle says, 'Hello I am a postman/ woman. My name is ... and I have letters for number ... and number ...' These two children stand and attempt to swap seats. At the same time the child in the middle tries to sit in one of the vacant seats. The child left without a seat goes into the middle.

Comments

Make sure that they take the number of their chair when they sit down.

Novelty names

Children enjoy the freshness of this game. Its underlying value is self-validation.

Resources

A list of suggested tones of voice; for example, as if you had been given a million pounds, as if you had jumped into an icy pool, as if you were squashed into a very small space, or as if you had a mouthful of hot potato. A blindfold is also needed.

What to do

Begin the game with a warm-up, asking the children to say their names as quickly as possible around the circle. Then choose a tone of voice from your list and ask them to repeat the round in that tone of voice. Try this for several tones.

Choose a child to wear the blindfold. This child (A) stands in the centre of the circle while the other children walk round the edge. When you call 'Stop' all the children stand still, the child in the centre carefully reaches out to touch another child, B, and asks, 'What's my name?' B says A's name and A has to guess who B is. If the guess is correct, they change places. If it is incorrect, the game continues and A moves on to a different child, until they guess correctly.

Finish the game by asking the children to choose a name they would like to give themselves, and ask for volunteers to share their choices with the rest of the group.

Comments

Before the children reveal the name they have chosen, remind the group that no negative comments are allowed in the circle. It may be a good idea to have a discussion about name calling to explore how hurtful this can be and to imagine how the children would feel if it were done to them.

Sharks and fish

This game creates a positive feeling within the group as the children talk about the things they really enjoy doing. It allows the children to learn more about one another and to appreciate their similarities and differences.

Resources

None. This game needs to be played in a large area with plenty of room to run around in.

What to do

Choose two children to be sharks; the rest of the children will be fish. Mark an area of the room that is home. The fish swim around the room holding their arms by their sides and flapping their hands as gills, whilst opening and closing their mouths. The sharks wait by the side. When you blow a whistle or shout 'Sharks', the fish must try to get home while the sharks attempt to catch them. The sharks mime their powerful jaws by opening and closing their arms in front of them as they run about. They catch a fish by touching their back. A fish that is caught becomes a shark in the next round until all the fish have been captured.

At the end call the children into a circle and ask them what they enjoyed about this game. Ask them to think of other games that they enjoy playing. The children take turns to complete the sentence, 'What I enjoy playing most is ... because ...', giving one reason for their choice. You can use a 'talking object' for this activity.

Comments

If a child has a particularly unusual or interesting variation of this game you might like to invite other children to ask for further information.

Jigsaws

This game encourages every child to develop a sense of value within the group.

Resources

Postcards – you need one for every five children in the group. Cut each into five pieces and write A on the back of the pieces in the first set, B on the second, and so on.

What to do

Shuffle the pieces and give one to each child. Explain that every piece has a letter on the back. Without talking, they must find the other children with the same letter and then put the pieces together to make the postcard. The first team to finish is the winner.

Comments

This is a fun and frantic game as the teams of children try to complete their jigsaws first. This type of activity is a good way of obtaining random groupings. You can continue with more team games or drama activities, or play the game again.

Paper, scissors, rock – with hands and feet!

This game gives each child an equal start.

Resources

None

What to do

Choose one child to begin the game. This child plays with the child on their left. All the children count to 3, and then the two children make paper (flat hand), scissors (index and middle finger held like open scissors) or rock (clenched fist). One is declared the winner; the rules are that paper wraps rock, scissors cut paper and rock blunts scissors. If they make the same action, they have another turn. The eventual winner moves on to the next child on their left. The play continues around the circle until it arrives back at the start.

Comments

Make this game even more fun by asking the children to stand and do the actions with their legs instead – paper (legs together), scissors (legs apart) and rock (crouched down). On the count of 3 the children jump into the air and take up their positions on landing.

The magician's wish

This game creates and enhances a feel-good atmosphere within the group. Imaginations have free rein, creating fun and enjoyment for all concerned.

Resources

A special wand

What to do

The children are asked to imagine that they are magicians who can wish for anything for the group. Encourage the children to be inventive. Each child completes the sentence, 'I wish that …' when it is their turn to hold the wand.

Comments

This game can lead to the children producing a wish list that could include gifts they would like to give, skills they would like others to possess and feelings they would like them to experience. Focusing on positive thoughts within the group creates companionship and healthy dynamics. This game is fun and very inviting to more withdrawn children.

Remote control

This game promotes self-awareness, requiring children to listen and act on instructions.

Resources

A remote control

What to do

Explain to the children that you have a remote control that tells them how to move. Your control has the following buttons on it:

Play – walk forward at a normal pace

Fast forward – run on the spot

Rewind – walk backwards carefully

Pause – stop briefly

Slow-motion – walk forwards slowly

Stop – end game

Call out instructions for the children to follow.

Comments

By using the *Pause* or *Slow-motion* button you can control the level of activity – if children become overexcited, you can calm them down. Let the children have a turn at giving instructions once they have the necessary self-control.

Monarch of the realm

This is a game that is fun and provides a positive focus on each child.

Resources

A paper or plastic crown and a blank scroll

What to do

Tell the children to imagine they are the monarch of the realm and they can issue any royal decree they like. This can be as preposterous as they wish; the object is to use their imaginations and have fun. You might like to give a few examples, such as:

I am Queen of the realm and I decree that all my subjects must wear pink woolly hats every Thursday.

I am King of the realm and I decree that all my subjects must eat pilchards and marmalade for breakfast.

Each child says their decree when the crown and scroll are passed to them.

Comments

This is a good activity for raising spirits and injecting a little enjoyment into a dull day. You can, if you wish, continue the game into a more serious area by discussing the real responsibilities of monarchs, and then exploring responsibilities the children have and how they deal with them.

Spin the bottle

This game encourages children to focus on their positive aspects. Saying good things about oneself is often difficult. However, it is important for sound self-esteem to be able to recognise your positive qualities and have others acknowledge them too.

Resources

An empty plastic bottle

What to do

The children take turns to spin the bottle. Whoever the neck of the bottle is pointing at when it stops says one thing they really enjoy doing that they are good at.

Comments

If you feel the game would take too long and you have a teaching assistant or other adult helper, you can divide the class into two.

My pet moans

This game begins to help children learn how to deal with things that they don't like in their lives. How far you wish to develop the activity will depend on the maturity of the group.

Resources

A flipchart and pen

What to do

Ask the children to brainstorm all the things that they dislike. These 'moans' can include foods, activities or objects such as spiders. Write all these on a flipchart. Ask the children what they would like to do with all of them; for example, put them in a bin bag and throw them away, bury them deep in the ground, drop them into the deepest ocean. You can ask the group to vote for one moan, but not the one they suggested, to see which is the class moan.

Comments

You can develop this game by asking the group to consider real ways of dealing with things that they don't like. Sometimes this might need courage, honesty or self-discipline. You may want to introduce a topic that is relevant to your group, such as bullying, or invite the children to raise an issue that affects them. If this happens, it is important that the children are instructed not to name others in a negative way. They can talk about the issues concerned, but not the people involved. If something is raised that you think is too delicate for general discussion, you can arrange a private meeting away from group.

Further activities

Something I am proud of

Cut individual bricks out of card and give one to each child. Ask each child to write their name on their brick and something they have done that they are proud of. This could be a good piece of work at school, a physical achievement like learning to swim or a kind act. Use the bricks to build a house or a wall as a display.

My flag

Give the children a large piece of paper each and tell them that they are going to make flags about themselves. They could divide the flags into four sections and decide what theme each section will have. Examples are: my family, what I enjoy doing, things I am good at, my favourite meal. Ask the children to draw and write in each section.

Stars in the night sky

Cut out a star for each child. They should be large enough for the children to write their name and a sentence on. Invite the children to write down one thing that they have achieved during the week. This may relate to work, a physical activity or behaviour. Make a display of the stars on a black background.

Portrait gallery

The children either draw a self-portrait or provide a photograph, which they stick onto a large piece of card. Invite them to write positive statements about themselves around the portrait and then display it.

Thumbprints

The children make thumbprints on paper. They compare their prints to see how each one is different and unique. Ask the children to turn their thumbprints into funny animals using felt pens.

Working in pairs within a group

Working with a partner can be less intimidating than being the focus of the whole group. Away from the limelight, shyer children can relax and gain confidence in their ability to contribute effectively. They can also share any group focus with another individual. Paired work makes it easier for all children to share ideas and be fully involved. Try to ensure that the children work with as many different partners as possible, so that they begin to feel comfortable with everyone in the group. Use some of the games in this book to pair children up in enjoyable ways.

Matching pairs

This game introduces the idea of similarities and differences between people; it is useful for introducing children to working in a pair.

Resources

Pairs of matched cards, enough for each child to have one. You could use picture cards (see page 126) for younger children and playing cards for older children.

What to do

Shuffle the cards and give them out. If you have an uneven number of children, take a card yourself too. Tell the children that they must find their partner, who will have a matching card. When they have found their partner, each pair must discover one meal they both really like. As soon as they have done this, they sit down together and fold their arms to show that they are ready. Collect the cards, give them another shuffle and then redistribute them. Tell the children to find their new partners and discover an animal they both like.

Comments

You can choose categories that are age-related, such as films, pop stars or books.

Scrambled stories

This game fosters cooperation with a partner. The children
will need to use language skills, imagination and
concentration.

Resources

Sequences of six illustrations that depict a story (see pages 127 and
128) – You will need enough copies of these for each pair to have a
set.

What to do

Give each pair a shuffled set of illustrations. Ask the children to put
the illustrations in the correct sequence to tell a story. When they
have completed this task, ask one pair to tell their story. Give other
pairs an opportunity to tell their story.

Comments

Children may like to make up their own sequences to use for this
game too.

You make me laugh

This game enables children to gain confidence in their abilities. It is fun and good for raising the spirits on a dull day.

Resources

None

What to do

Divide the children into pairs. Tell the children that they have to take it in turns to try to make their partner laugh. They can pull funny faces or tell jokes, but they must not use physical contact. Their partner must try to remain serious for as long as possible. They can play this game several times; changing partners each time.

Comments

If children find it hard to concentrate they could read whilst their partner tries to attract their attention.

Write a list of all the things that make the children laugh. You could also arrange a joke time when the children can share their favourites.

Mirror, mirror

This game promotes cooperation by requiring children to focus carefully on their partners.

Resources

None

What to do

Tell the children to stand close together, with each child facing their partner. Each child will take a turn at leading the actions while their partner tries to mirror them exactly. Tell the children to begin their movements slowly, then speed up a bit once their partners have become more confident.

Comments

With experience children can introduce subtle movements, such as a change of expression or moving one finger. Discuss with the children how they found the game and what was the most difficult aspect of it. You could let the children work out a short mirroring routine with their partners to see how exactly they can match their movements.

Hand writing

This game develops close paired work involving concentration and touch.

Resources

None

What to do

The children take it in turns to close their eyes; their partner then slowly writes a word on their palm with one finger. Tell the children to begin with simple three-letter words and to make the finger writing very clear and exact. The child with their eyes closed has to guess the word. They can ask for it to be repeated if they did not understand it the first time.

Comments

A variation on this game is to have a child wearing a blindfold sitting in the centre of the circle. Someone is quietly chosen to write their name on the child's palm. If the child correctly guesses the identity of the writer from their name they swap places; if not another writer is chosen.

Yes or no

Yes or no

This game encourages language skills and imaginative thought. It helps the children to focus on relevant questions and to categorise information.

Resources

A set of cards with common objects shown in words or illustrations (see pages 126 and 129)

What to do

One child from each pair collects a card, which they must not let their partner see. Their partner must try to guess the object on the card by asking questions about it, but they only receive yes or no answers. When they have guessed correctly, a new card is picked and the roles are reversed.

Comments

It is a good idea to begin this game by talking through the sort of questions that will help the children make correct guesses. Some will need a clue.

Find the headline

This imaginative game is good for cooperation, language skills and assessing visual cues.

Resources

You will need appropriate newspaper or magazine illustrations with bold headlines for each pair.

What to do

Prior to the lesson, cut off the headlines and keep them separate. Give each pair an illustration and place all the headlines in the centre of the circle. Tell the children they must find the correct headline for their illustration and then try to work out the story behind it.

Comments

You can play the game in reverse by giving the children the headline and asking them to find the correct illustration. You could also give illustrations and ask the children to write their own headlines. Discuss with them how headlines are meant to grab the reader's attention and how they must bear this in mind when writing their own.

A picture paints a thousand words

This game develops language skills and imaginative thought.
The children have great fun playing it.

Resources

A selection of nouns written on slips of paper; you will need three
for each pair in the group (see page 130). Also a flipchart and pen.

What to do

Invite each pair to take three slips of paper. Tell the children that
they must make up an interesting sentence using their three words.
When they have all completed this task, invite the children back to
the circle. The pairs take turns to draw on the flipchart and mime
their sentences for the others to guess.

Comments

Make sure that the children realise they must include all their words
in just one sentence. You can also use the slips to see which pair can
make the longest or funniest sentence.

Lead me home

This game develops a sense of peer support
and confidence in a group. The children need to
listen carefully.

Resources

Three blindfolds

What to do

Ask the children in pairs, to think of a sound that they can practise
and recognise. Ask for three sets of pairs who would like to go into
the centre of the circle. One child in each pair puts on a blindfold.
Their partners then move away and stand in a gap in the circle. On
a signal, these children call to their partner using the sound they
have chosen. The children wearing the blindfolds listen for their
partner's call and move carefully about the circle until they have
located them. The other children gently keep them inside the circle.
Continue like this until all the children have had a turn.

Comments

If you feel brave, can stand the noise and know that your children
will be sensible, you could try this with the whole class. You may
play this game with clapped sequences instead of spoken calls.

Sausage

This game encourages concentration and inventiveness, and is great fun to play.

Resources

A stopwatch or egg-timer

What to do

Ask the children to sit opposite each other in pairs. For two to three minutes, one child asks their partner questions to which they have to reply 'Sausage'. The object of the game is to make their partner laugh and gain a point; so the more bizarre the question the better. You can give them some examples, such as:

What is the name of your girlfriend?

What do you brush your teeth with?

What is that coming out of your ear?

The children can change partners and play the game several times to see who can score the most points.

Comments

You could play this game as a knockout challenge to find the Champion Sausage, winners from each round going through to the next.

Robots

This game develops trust and cooperation. The children must use imagination and concentration.

Resources

None, but a large space with sufficient room for the children to work in is advisable.

What to do

One child from each pair is a robot. Tell the other child in the pair that they are going to direct the robot. You can give examples of appropriate instructions, such as: walk three paces forward, turn left, pretend you are climbing stairs, stop and sit on the floor cross-legged.

Comments

You could develop this game by asking the children to write out specific step-by-step directions to get from one place to another in the building. They can then arrange a time to try these out with you.

Double talk

This game is an enjoyable way to develop
listening skills.

Resources

You could use prepared scripts if you think the children will have
difficulty in ad-libbing.

What to do

Tell the children they are going to take turns to talk while their
partners try to copy their speech as simultaneously as possible.
Warn the children not to let their voices become too loud. When
they have agreed what they will say and have practised it, ask if
any pair would like to demonstrate.

Comments

You can develop the theme of listening by talking about what the
children think they need to do to listen well. Ask them to be very
quiet and note all the noises that they usually filter out.
Alternatively, listen to four or five speeches at the same time
and then ask the children what they can remember of each one.

Secret sketching

This game promotes careful listening, concentration and language skills.

Resources

Paper and pencils

What to do

Pairs sit back to back. One of each pair does a simple line drawing for their partner. They then give their partner specific instructions on how to reproduce the drawing. At the end the children compare their drawings to see how similar they are. They then reverse roles.

Comments

It may be a good idea to demonstrate the concept first if working with less mature children. Discuss with the children what they found the most difficult, giving or receiving instructions and when they really needed to concentrate. You could develop this theme by asking the children to write out step-by-step instructions for a simple task, such as making a cup of tea or washing their hair.

Blindfold alley

This is a good game for developing trust and cooperation. The children consider the welfare of their partners and experience what it is like to trust their own welfare to others.

Resources

Some blindfolds and a selection of objects to use as obstacles

What to do

Set up an obstacle course in a straight line or circle. Make sure that it is fairly easy to negotiate and decide with the children whether they will step over or go round each obstacle. Tell the children that one child in each pair will wear a blindfold. The children wearing blindfolds must be carefully led through the obstacle course by their partners. The guides can use verbal instructions or hold their partner's hand. At the end of the course they swap roles.

Comments

Make sure the children adopt a responsible attitude towards leading their partners. They should not proceed too quickly, and must stop if their partners feel nervous and need to regain their confidence. Discuss with the children how they felt in either role and what gave them confidence both to lead and be led; did the children who led first appreciate what it felt like to be led before they had their turn? This can be a good opening to discuss empathy, and how it can be difficult to understand how others feel when we have not shared their experiences.

Tall stories

This is an enjoyable way to encourage communication skills and concentration.

Resources

None

What to do

Ask the children, in pairs, to think of a well-known story. They each tell their story to the other at the same time. They must try to make their own story so exciting and interesting that their partner stops talking to listen. If they do that, they get a point. The children swap partners and play again. At the end, see who has the most points and is the Champion Storyteller.

Comments

Warn the children before you play this game that it is not about who can shout the loudest; they must use interest, not volume, to capture their partner's attention. Discuss with the children what helped them to block out the other children's stories.

Further activities

Body drawings

Using large sheets of paper, children take turns to lie down while their partner draws around their body outline. These can be cut out and displayed.

Special occasion cards

The children work in pairs to produce a card for a special occasion of their choice. Ask them to pay particular attention to the message they write inside.

Posters

Each child makes a poster depicting all their partner's good qualities. Encourage the children to think of catchy slogans to include on the poster.

Dilemmas

List a selection of moral dilemmas on a flipchart. These could include: you see a friend stealing something from a shop, you witness a bullying incident in the playground, a friend has run away from home and you know where she is, a friend has cheated in a test. Make the situations age appropriate. The children choose a dilemma to explore in their pairs. They can share their decisions with the rest of the group at the end.

Comic strips

Collect a selection of comics for pairs to look through. Ask them to pay attention to the characters and the language. Let them devise a comic strip of their own. They can either invent their characters or use themselves in the story. Tell them to produce about six pictures for their story.

Building a group identity

The games in this section encourage the individual child to become an integrated member of the group. They enhance group dynamics, creating positive responses for each child in the group.

Matching bricks

This game promotes goodwill and friendship within the group as children search for the other members of their set. The competitive element is an incentive to encourage the children to be cooperative, even with children they aren't particularly friendly with.

Resources

A bag containing five or six sets of different-coloured bricks

What to do

Ask each child to take a brick out of the bag without looking. When all the children have a brick, tell them they must get together in groups of matching colours, hold hands in a circle and sit down. The first group to sit down wins. Collect the bricks in, give the bag a shake and play again.

Comments

You can make the final collection of bricks more fun by asking each group to move in a different way when they return their bricks.

Softball challenge

This game involves concentration and observation. The whole group is drawn into the activity.

Resources

A sponge ball

What to do

Practise throwing the ball from child to child to make sure the circle is the right size. Pick a theme, such as items for a picnic or names of pop groups. As each child receives the ball they say something linked to that theme. They can say 'Pass' if they are stuck for an idea.

Comments

You can roll the ball with children whose throwing and catching skills are not well developed.

A round of applause

It is good to receive the positive affirmation of one's peers and this game provides an opportunity for this. For some children such chances may not occur very often.

Resources

Each child will need to have a different rehearsed sentence to say. It could relate to a topic that you are studying or be a sentence from their work. Younger children could show a piece of work they are proud of.

What to do

Each child stands up in turn and says their sentence. At the end of each contribution everyone shows their appreciation by clapping enthusiastically.

Comments

Look for other ways and opportunities for the children to applaud their peers. This is often much more meaningful to a child than adult praise and can have a very positive impact.

Happy families

This enjoyable game creates a sense of belonging as the children claim membership of a particular group. It is also good for observation and concentration.

Resources

A set of cards consisting of family groups, such as animal groups, mathematical shapes, colours or leaf shapes (see page 131). You could also use playing cards, matching the numbers, or a set of Happy Families.

What to do

Show the cards to the children so that they are familiar with the different family groups. Give each child a card. Tell them that when you give the signal they are to move around the centre of the circle, exchanging their cards as many times as possible. When you say 'Stop' they must find the other members of their family group as quickly and silently as possible.

Comments

This game can provide a suitable starting point for looking at different groups in society, especially if your children are from different ethnic backgrounds. It provides a positive experience for any child who feels isolated because of cultural differences.

Alibis

This game encourages the children to work together to achieve a goal.

Resources

A flipchart with 20 lines on it, to represent 20 points, and a pen

What to do

Before the game, take four children aside, who wouldn't normally work together, and tell them that they are going to be accused of a crime. They must work out detailed alibis for the time of the crime. Give them 15 minutes to prepare their story in a quiet corner of the room. The nature of the crime can be as outlandish as you like; for example, putting a bucket of water above the door, so that the water falls on the teacher's head.

The rest of the class is a team of detectives who will question the four suspects to try to find inconsistencies in their accounts. Before beginning the game, find a safe place outside the room for the suspects to await questioning. Begin by inviting the first suspect into the circle. The detectives ask questions relating to the offence, they must remember the answers they are given. The second suspect is invited in and questioned. Each time their answer does not match the first suspect's account, a point is crossed off the flipchart. However, the same detail cannot be counted as an inconsistency twice. For example, if suspect number 2 got the time wrong, this detail cannot be used to score more points with the third and fourth suspects. The detectives have to think of new questions to create more opportunities to catch the suspects out. If the suspects lose their 20 points, they go to prison and the game is over.

Comments

Once each suspect has been questioned, it is a good idea for them to face away from the circle so that they can listen, but not give any visual signals to the remaining suspects.

Shake a word

This game uses language skills to focus on cooperation and observation.

Resources

Break down compound words with two components into their separate entities and print them on different coloured cards so that you end up with two sets; for example, bath/room, tooth/brush, shoe/lace, sea/shore, hand/brake, cup/board, week/end, day/light, door/bell, sun/shine, book/case, wood/land, rail/way, hop/scotch, centi/pede. Always put the first word on one colour and the second on a different colour.

What to do

Mix up the cards and give them out, one to each child. Explain to the children what the cards represent and tell them that the object of the game is to try to find the child with the word that fits their's and enables them to make a compound word.

Comments

Try to avoid choosing words that could be matched in ways you did not intend. If you end up with children who cannot find a suitable partner, ask the other pairs to read out their compound words. You may find that you have a pair who have made a viable word, but it is not the one that you intended. If this happens, commend them for producing a correct word, but explain that they will have to swap partners so that everyone can find a match.

Question time

This is a useful game for making sure that every child is included in the circle activity. It is a good one to use when you want shyer children to gain confidence in speaking in front of their peers.

Resources

A flipchart and pen, and some slips of paper with the children's names on them.

What to do

Ask the children to brainstorm a list of general questions, such as:

> *What is your favourite meal/TV programme/*
> *pop star/hobby?*
>
> *Where would you like to visit?*
>
> *What famous person would you like to meet?*
>
> *What would you really like to buy?*

Write these questions on the flipchart. Give out the slips of paper so that each child has someone else's name. The children take turns around the circle to choose a question from the list to ask the child named on their slip of paper, beginning the question with that child's name.

Comments

Take care when compiling the list that you do not include any questions relating to sensitive issues.

A friendly bunch

This game fosters group cooperation. The aim is to get children to mix well in groups that do not necessarily contain their usual friends.

Resources

None

What to do

Tell the children that they are to mingle in the middle of the circle. You will call a number from 2 to 5 and the children must get into groups of that number. They must not stop to look for their friends, but form groups with the nearest people as quickly as possible.

Comments

You can develop this game by asking the children to create a tableau each time they form a new group. This could be a hospital scene, a restaurant, a dog show or a pop concert. When you call 'Freeze', they must stand still in their scene.

The global village

This game encourages the children to work together to achieve their goals.

Resources

None, but plenty of room to run in is necessary

What to do

The game begins with a king or queen, who stands facing away from the other children. The rest of the children decide on a country and a mime to represent it; for example, Australia – a kangaroo, Spain – a bullfighter, America – a baseball player. The children then go up to the king or queen, who now faces them, and say, 'We've come to see Your Majesty.' The king or queen asks, 'Which country do you come from?' The children perform their mime and the monarch guesses the country. When a correct guess is made, the children shout 'Yes' and run for home. The king or queen chases them and any children tagged become kings or queens in the next round. The king or queen may make three guesses. If they still cannot arrive at the right country the children shout its name and run for home in the same way. The game continues until all the children are caught.

Comments

It might be a good idea to think of some countries and suitable mimes before you play this game, especially with younger children. The children deciding on the country and mime must do this very quietly if the monarchs are in the same room.

Our gifts to you

The children consider their peers, making a positive approach to them. This game creates a good atmosphere within the group and a positive focus on each individual.

Resources

A piece of paper and a pencil for each child and a box or bag

What to do

Ask the children to write their name on their piece of paper. Collect in the names and place them in the box or bag. One at a time, take a name out and invite the children to put their hand up to volunteer a gift they would like to give that person. Choose three children to say what they would give. Encourage the children to be imaginative in their choices; for example, a safari in Africa, a ride in a hot-air balloon, a robot to do all their homework, a diamond necklace.

Comments

With older children you might like to ask them to make the gifts more abstract; for example, wisdom, the ability to fly or the ability to talk to animals.

At the end of term the children may make small beautiful boxes. They write their gifts for each other on separate gift tags and post them in the appropriate boxes, so that the children all have something to keep forever.

Treasured words

In this game each child has a turn at receiving positive attention from the group.

Resources

Paper, pens and a box or bag

What to do

Write the children's names on slips of paper and place them in a box or bag. Take the names out one at a time and ask the children to put their hands up and say something positive about that person. The positive statements might mention such things as: being helpful, being friendly, having a nice smile, something that child is good at. Choose three volunteers for each child.

Comments

If you think there are children in your group whom the others might have difficulty finding positive statements for, make an effort to praise those children in front of the rest of the group prior to this game. With some groups it might also be a good idea to brainstorm the positive qualities that we look for in people before you begin.

Follow the thread

Using a ball of ribbon around the circle helps to bind the group together, practically and psychologically. All the children are involved and encouraged to feel a sense of belonging.

Resources

A ball of ribbon or string

What to do

Tell the children to imagine they are going on a journey together. They are going to travel to somewhere warm and sunny by the sea. Ask them to think of one thing that they would like to take with them; it may be something for the journey or for their destination, something to use or wear, or for leisure. They must wait their turn to speak to say it aloud. Give the ball of string to one child. Ask them to say what they would take. This child then holds onto the end of the string, passing the ball on to the next child. The ball is passed around the circle. As each child passes it on they continue to hold the string itself. When the ball has travelled round the circle all the children should be holding the string. The first child then winds the string back onto the ball. Younger children can sing a song while this is happening. Older children can play a word association game.

Comments

This process can be used for all sorts of activities, such as rounds, storytelling and brainstorming. It helps children to concentrate and anticipate their turn. You can also pass the string randomly across the circle, asking children to raise their hands to answer, creating an interesting web effect. Take care where you step as the web gets more complex.

Sticky treats

This game uses affirmation to promote positive feelings within the group.

Resources

Three coloured sticky dots for each child

What to do

Each child is given three sticky dots. They place these on the hands of any three children they choose and say something positive about each child. Each child needs to end up with three stickers awarded by other children.

Comments

If you have any children in your group that you think the other children may be unwilling to award stickers to, it may be wise to talk about the aim of the game prior to starting. Let the children know that it is to create a positive feeling for all the children as this is good for developing a happy atmosphere within the group. The game will then be carried out in a spirit of generosity.

Hidden treasure

This game is fun and involves the whole group working together.

Resources

A blindfold and a small object to hide

What to do

One child is blindfolded for a moment whilst the object is hidden. The child's blindfold is then removed and they are invited to search for the object. They are guided by the other children's clapping, which is quiet when the child is a long way from the object, but gets louder as the child gets nearer.

Comments

You can play this game with all kinds of different instructions: the clapping could be slow, becoming faster; the children could hum quietly or loudly or they could tap or stamp their feet. Children will enjoy thinking up their own instructions too.

A variation on this game involves the blindfolded child sitting on a chair guarding some treasure, such as a bunch of keys, in the centre of the circle. A chosen child tries to creep up and take the treasure. If the blindfolded child hears a noise and successfully points to the child approaching, that child returns to their seat and another child is chosen. If the treasure is captured a new guard is chosen.

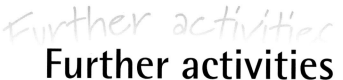

Further activities

Achievement board

Use this board to display special things to do with a particular child, such as pieces of work, photos and positive comments from other children.

Wheel of fortune

Let the children make wheels out of card. The wheels should have eight spokes on them. Ask the children to write eight good things that have happened to them along the spokes. Display the wheels.

A perfect afternoon

Ask the children to plan their perfect afternoon, including where they would be, what they would do and whom they would be with. They can then choose a partner to share their plans with.

Feeling good

Get the children to brainstorm all the things that make them feel good. These may include concrete things such as new clothes or going to the cinema, and abstract ones such as someone praising them or their doing something well. Make a wall display with all the things listed.

Myself, my feelings

The games in this section look at various aspects of emotional well-being. They encourage the children to think about body language and the value of being able to read that of others. They also focus on the similarities and differences between individuals and help the children develop empathy. Finally, they celebrate the value and uniqueness of each child.

Clockwork toys

This game provides an enjoyable introduction to looking at body rhythms and feelings related to them.

Resources

None

What to do

Tell the children they are to pretend to be wind-up toys. They have just been wound up and they can move around until their mechanisms run down. They will gradually move more and more slowly until they stop. Let the children repeat this two or three times then come back to the circle. Ask them to think of times during the day when their bodies are full of energy or slowing down, and how they feel at such times. Explore what they do when they feel run down; for example, eat a meal when they are hungry, sleep when they are tired, exercise when they feel lethargic.

Comments

Talk to the children about other times when their bodies feel run down; for example, when it is a hot day, when they are ill, after strenuous exercise. Ask the children why they think this happens.

Actions speak louder than words

In this game the children investigate the spoken and physical language of feelings.

Resources

None

What to do

Give each group of five or six children an emotion – such as happy, sad, angry, frightened. Tell the children to pretend it is the birthday of one person in their group. Each group must work out a short scene where they are all at that person's party, but they can only behave with the emotion their group has been given. Allow 10 to 15 minutes for this and then ask the groups to show their scenes to the others. Afterwards explore the clues that indicated which emotion the different groups were trying to convey.

Comments

You could develop this game by asking the children to think of different emotions and perform mimed scenes for these.

Guess the venue

This game enables the children to look at how we convey our feelings through our actions.

Resources

Write a selection of events and associated feelings on a flipchart, for example:

> *Watching a football match – show enjoyment and appreciation*
>
> *Entering a dark house – show nervousness and fear*
>
> *A war dance – show anger and bravado*
>
> *Waiting for a pop star to arrive – show excitement and anticipation*
>
> *Finding a lost child – show care and concern*

What to do

Sort the children into groups of five. Explain to them that they will quietly be given one event. They are to devise a mime for this that the other groups will try to guess. They must pay particular attention to miming the appropriate emotions and gestures. Spread the groups out and tell them to work quietly to avoid other groups overhearing. After 10 minutes, return to the circle and ask each group to perform their mime. Explore what each mime was and the clues that helped.

Comments

Just for fun, ask the children to work out a new mime for their event in which one or two of the children act with inappropriate emotions; for example, being sad at a party or being scared at a pop star's arrival. Ask them how this felt.

Living legends

This game provides a positive focus for each child as part of the whole.

Resources

None

What to do

Each child chooses an alliterative adjective to preface their name. Explain that the description should be positive; for example, friendly Fiona, kind Karl, marvellous Mary, wonderful Wayne. Ask for volunteers to begin the game, so that the more confident children show the others what to do. Each child is then asked to introduce themselves with an accompanying symbolic gesture. For example, joyful John might open his arms and jump with joy. The other children say the child's name in the same tone of voice and copy their gesture.

Comments

Make sure all the children are able to think of a suitable word; if they are stuck ask the other children for suggestions.

The wrong job

The wrong job

This game uses imagination and mime to explore
body language.

Resources

None

What to do

Choose a child to begin the game. Explain to the children that they
are going to mime an action, but when they are asked what they are
doing they will say a *different* action, which must then be mimed by
the next child and so on. For example:

> *Child 1: Mimes washing up.*
>
> *Child 2:* What are you doing?
>
> *Child 1:* Scrubbing the floor.
>
> *Child 2: Mimes scrubbing the floor.*
>
> *Child 3:* What are you doing?
>
> *Child 2:* Making a cake.
>
> *Child 3: Mimes making a cake.*

Comments

Talk to the children about telling lies. Whilst this may be acceptable
in a game where the children know the rules, it is not considered
acceptable in general life. Ask the children to think of all the
reasons why people should be truthful and record their answers
on a flipchart.

Back to the start

This game involves using facial expression and tone of voice to convey information. The children have to read the messages they are given by their partner's actions.

Resources

A list of incidents on individual cards (see pages 132 and 133) and some sticky tape

What to do

Each child has an incident stuck to their back. In pairs the children read their partner's incident silently. They take it in turns to describe it to their partner through mime and facial expression.

If you think your group is able to do this, ask them to use gibberish as speech. The children have to guess their incident; they can ask questions of their partner, but all replies must be in gibberish. Younger children can receive yes or no answers. Once a child has guessed correctly, they change roles with their partner.

Comments

Discuss with the children how much the tone of voice and facial expressions helped them discover their incidents. Explore what they could guess about the incidents from these two factors.

Puzzling looks

Puzzling looks

This game encourages concentration skills.

Resources

None

What to do

Number the children around the circle. Explain to the children that when you call their number they must answer 'Yes'. No other child is allowed to speak. Each time you call a number you look at a different child; for example, you call 2, but look at child 12; or you call 23, but look at child 17. The children must remain alert and refrain from speaking. They will find it hard not to say something when you look at the wrong child. Once the children have practised the game, speed up the action. If a child does not respond to their number, the children either side can gently whisper to them.

Comments

Talk to the children about their feelings during this game. Were any of them nervous about missing their number? How did they feel if they did miss their number? Lead the children to respond with 'I felt embarrassed when ...' Discuss any situations when they have not responded correctly. Talk about being considerate to others by prompting or showing them how to respond.

You choose

This game explores the concept of tolerance. It also focuses on, and celebrates, the differences between individuals.

Resources

A questionnaire with tick boxes for each child (see pages 134 and 135) and pencils

What to do

Give out the questionnaire and ask the children to tick their responses to each question. You might want to read through the questions together beforehand. In a circle compare and discuss their responses. Explore why some people have made different choices. Talk about how such things as family background, peer pressure and fashion have an influence on people's choices.

Comments

Talk to the children about the importance of accepting and valuing the differences between people. Tolerance leads to harmony and peace, whilst intolerance leads to conflict.

Pavement reporter

This game focuses the children's attention on the range of feelings about an issue within a group.

Resources

Cards marked with the numbers 1 to 5, and a selection of contentious statements such as:

There should be no chips on the lunch menu

Homework should be abolished

Children under the age of 16 shouldn't be allowed mobile phones

Footballers shouldn't be paid so much money

We shouldn't have kings and queens any more

What to do

Agree an imaginary line along the length of the classroom to represent a pavement. Place the five numbered cards evenly along this line. After reading a statement ask the children to stand by the number that represents their opinion. The five numbers represent:

1. Strongly agree with statement
2. Agree with statement
3. Neither agree nor disagree with statement
4. Disagree with statement
5. Strongly disagree with statement

Choose a reporter each time you read a statement to ask two or three of the children for their views.

Comments

Make sure that the children are clear about which number to choose. Talk to them about why people have different views and feelings and the importance of tolerance.

Plus points

This game focuses on the children's strengths and weaknesses, helping them to appreciate that people have different strengths and that they are all valuable.

Resources

A pencil and a copy of a list of contrasting character traits for each child (see page 136)

What to do

The children make a mark along the line between the pairs of character traits. The position will indicate how far each child identifies with one word in the pair. Let the children compare their responses with their neighbours in the circle.

Comments

Talk to the children about the value of different strengths; for example, there is a place in society for both the tortoise and the hare. Everybody has some strengths, even though they may be less visible than others. Ask the children to consider which of their character traits they think of as weaknesses. Explore how others might see them as strengths and how they could change to see them in this light.

Further activities

Mood doodles

Ask the children to draw abstract lines, circles and squiggles to represent different moods; for example, happy, sad, angry, nervous.

Similarities and differences

Ask the children to draw bar charts to represent different surveys carried out about the group; for example, appearance (hair colour, height, shoe size), favourite subject/meal, what pets they have.

Mood weather charts

Ask the children to draw weather symbols and link them to different moods; for example, sun – happy, storm – temper, rain – sad, wind – restless.

Goalposts

Make a large display of a set of goalposts. Cut out paper circles for balls. Give one to each child and ask them to write a goal they would like to achieve in school on their ball. Line up the balls in front of the goal. When a child has achieved their target let them place their ball in the goal.

Hurt feelings

Brainstorm all the things that hurt the children's feelings. Ask them how they react when their feelings are hurt. Ask them to think of the best way to react.

Tonics

Ask the children to think up amusing tonics to give to someone who is feeling sad. Tell them to be really imaginative about their ingredients. If necessary, give examples such as a ray of sunshine, cool sea breeze, birdsong.

Thinking and concentrating

The games in this section focus on thinking
and concentration skills, which aid success and
positive self-esteem. The group games also provide
a focus on cooperation and the sharing of
knowledge and experience.

Birthday game

This game develops thinking and concentration skills.

Resources

Two sets of 12 cards. Write a month of the year on each card in the first set. Write a different activity on each card in the second set; for example, change seats, count backwards from 10, hop around the circle, curl up into a ball. Put the sets of cards into two containers.

What to do

First make sure all the children know the month of their birth. A child takes a card from the month container and reads it out. All the children with a birthday in that month stand up. A volunteer then takes a card from the activity container and those children perform that activity.

Comments

The children could make a block graph to see how their birthdays are spread over the year. They might like to choose an appropriate symbol to represent each month; for example, January – a snowflake, October – an autumn leaf, November – a firework. You could also discuss with the children the reasons why we celebrate birthdays.

Time capsules

In this game the children reflect on what is important in their lives and what objects represent their lifestyles. They must work cooperatively and act on the consensus.

Resources

Paper and pencils

What to do

Divide the children into groups of four or five. Ask them to imagine they are preparing a time capsule that will be buried for future generations. Tell them they can put ten items into the capsule, such as a hamburger, a video game, a scooter, a popular toy, a CD. Ask the children to brainstorm possible items. They can vote for the ten that they consider the most representative. They should then return to the circle to compare their findings with those of the other groups.

Comments

The groups might like to draw the contents of their time capsules for a display. They can also compare their capsules and find out what was the most popular item for the whole class.

Who am I?

Who am I?

This game helps to develop questioning skills as the children seek to guess their mysterious identities.

Resources

Sticky labels (one for each child in the group)

What to do

Brainstorm famous people that the children know well and write each name on a sticky label. Ask the children to stand facing away from you whilst you put a label on each back. The children take it in turns to guess who they are by asking the other children questions about themselves. You might like to limit them to ten questions to ensure everyone has a turn at guessing.

Comments

If you think your group may find this game difficult, spend some time beforehand discussing a range of famous people and write their names on a flipchart. Then help the children to consider the questions they could ask to find out who they are.

Animated alphabets

In this game the children need to use their imagination and cooperate with their group.

Resources

None

What to do

Divide the children into groups of five or six. Explain that you will call out a letter of the alphabet and they are to make a body sculpture of it in their groups. They can race to see which group can do this first.

Comments

You could give each group a different letter to make up a class word or try this with numerals, combining groups to make bigger amounts.

Free thoughts

The children work as a whole group to develop thinking and concentration skills. A competitive element can be introduced to add more fun to this game.

Resources

None

What to do

Tell the children that you will give them a word. They must think of a word associated with it and say it when it is their turn in the circle. Play a practice round. Choose another word and play round the circle again. Give the children words with plenty of associations, such as the sea, summer or school. You can add fun to the proceedings by timing each round. You could also allow children to say 'Challenge' if they do not think an association is valid. If the player cannot give a satisfactory explanation of the association they must try again.

Comments

If some children find this activity too difficult other group members can volunteer words for them.

First one back

In this game the children need to concentrate on what is happening and be ready to respond to a given signal.

Resources

None

What to do

For this game the chairs need to be pointing around the edge of the circle, rather than inwards. There must be one fewer chair than the number of children. One child begins the game by moving around the outside of the circle in a chosen manner, such as hopping, jumping or crawling. Don't allow them to move faster than a walk. This child taps four other children on the shoulder. They follow, copying the movement. When the leader shouts, 'Back to seats!' the children make their way as quickly as possible to the vacant seats. The child left standing becomes the new leader and must think of a different way to move. The other children can offer suggestions if they are asked.

Comments

If you would prefer, you can write ways of moving on slips of paper and place these in a box for the children to pick from. This can add to the enjoyment, as no one knows what they will get to do.

A hundred-year sleep

This game requires the children to use their knowledge and experience to make predictions.

Resources

None

What to do

Divide the children into small groups. Tell them to imagine they have just woken from a hundred-year sleep. They are to discuss the changes that have occurred since they fell asleep, deciding on the things they would be amazed, delighted or alarmed by. Ask the children to vote, in their groups, on the one thing they think would have the biggest impact on them. Call the groups back to the circle and ask each of them to mime one of the things they discussed for the others to guess.

Comments

You can develop this game by asking the children to imagine they will sleep for a hundred years from now. Ask them to discuss the world they think they would wake up to.

Machines

In this game the children work cooperatively in small groups, pooling their knowledge and ideas. This game requires planning so that each group member has an equal part to play.

Resources

None

What to do

Explain that in groups of four or five, the children are going to become parts of a machine. They must decide what their machine does; for example, it could be a machine to make ice cream or a machine that collects dead leaves from the garden. If you think some groups may have difficulty in thinking of a machine, you could brainstorm ideas with the children beforehand.

When they have decided what their machine will be, they must decide on its individual parts. They then have to coordinate these working parts into the whole machine. This can involve sounds, actions and parts working simultaneously or in sequence. When the children have practised their routine they can demonstrate and explain their machine to the other groups.

Comments

You can continue this theme of group work by asking the children to create group sculptures. Each member of the group becomes a part of the sculpture; for example, a tree, a bridge, a house, a park bench.

Guess what I am

In this game the children need to organise their thoughts systematically to help them make accurate interpretations.

Resources

A set of cards with everyday objects written on them (see page 137)

What to do

Each child is given a card. The children are allowed five minutes to think about how they will describe their object, without naming it. You can then ask for volunteers or go round the circle with each child describing their object and the other children guessing what it is.

Comments

This game can be played in pairs. When the children have guessed the objects, they can either find new partners or take different cards. You can limit questions to yes or no answers, or restrict the number of guesses, to keep the game flowing. The children may like to choose their own everyday objects to describe too.

Where will it all end?

This game focuses on language skills and imagination.

Resources

A list of unfinished sentences written on a flipchart, for example:

On Saturday I had a great surprise …

We were eating lunch when …

I answered the door and …

We were driving in the car when …

I heard a loud bang and saw …

The person turned round and …

When I entered the building …

What to do

The children either work individually or in pairs. Give them a sentence and ask them to try to think of an interesting ending. Allow a few minutes for them to work on this. The children then read their sentences around the circle. This can create hilarious results.

Comments

Choose an incomplete sentence and have fun brainstorming the different endings the children can think of. They might like to generate their own sentence beginnings too.

Shopping list

This game involves observation and
concentration skills.

Resources

None

What to do

Tell the children to think of an item that they would like to buy.
If they need ideas, say it could be something to eat, a toy, a CD or
some clothes. They must think of a suitable mime to demonstrate
their choice to the circle. Ask for volunteers to perform their mimes
for the others to guess. The children can say where they would buy
their item if they need to give a clue. If nobody can guess it after
three attempts, they must reveal what it was.

Comments

Play fast rounds going through the alphabet. Choose some items
and ask the children to guess how much they think they cost.

The truth will out

This game encourages thinking skills, group discussion and decision-making. It also provides an opportunity to introduce new vocabulary.

Resources

A selection of words with three definitions, only one of which is correct (see pages 138 and 139)

What to do

Ask for three volunteers to start the game. Each child reads a definition of the same word. The other children decide which they think is the true version and stand in front of that child. Once all the children have made their choices the volunteers reveal which of the three was the true definition. Repeat with a new word and three different children.

Comments

It is a good idea to say each word first, so that the children know the correct pronounciation. Prior to playing the game talk to the children about being careful to read all three definitions in the same manner; they must not give away the true definition by their tone of voice or facial expression. The children might enjoy making up some word cards of their own with the aid of a dictionary.

Further activities

The shape of words

Let the children have fun writing words in the shape of their meanings; for example, the letters of *balloon* could be written in a circle and the letters of *taller* could increase in height.

Something new

Ask the children to write down all the subjects they study in school. Tell them to write down one new thing they have learnt in each subject over the last week.

Life line

Ask the children to draw a horizontal line representing the years of their lives. Tell them to choose five different ages along the line and write down one bad and one good thing about being that age. In a circle compare and discuss their comments.

My home

Ask each child to draw the outline of their home on a large sheet of paper. Tell them to write in all the good things that can be found there, including both concrete and abstract items.

House rules

Ask the children to think of ten rules they would draw up if they were homeowners. Talk about these in a circle and ask the children to vote for the most important rule.

Job descriptions

Tell the children to think of a job they would like. Ask them to write a job description for it, taking into account the tasks involved and the personal qualities required to fill such a position.

Developing attention skills

The games in this section focus on observation skills and attention to detail. The children will develop the use of their senses and the ability to use knowledge and experience in imaginative ways. Such creative thinking will equip children to meet the challenges of life with confidence.

In the driving seat

This game develops observational skills and creative thinking.

Resources

A chair in the centre of the circle and a list of different seats (see page 140)

What to do

The children take turns to sit in the chair in the centre and mime sitting in a seat from the list. The other children try to guess what it is.

Comments

Children might enjoy thinking up their own list of seats. You could also use the chair in a miming game in which children pretend it is a different object; for example, a guitar, an umbrella, a lawnmower. The rest of the group try to guess the object.

The toyshop

This exciting game develops concentration and listening skills.

Resources

A music CD or a whistle, and a torch

What to do

Each child pretends to be a toy in a toyshop – for example, a teddy, a doll, an animal, a vehicle, a ball. They take up a position as their toy. When they hear the music or the whistle, they come to life and move around appropriately. When the music stops or the whistle is blown, they return to their starting positions. You then shine the torch on a child, who must come to life in the spotlight. Do this with several children.

Comments

You could finish this game by playing musical statues.

Discuss why the children have toys, and what they can learn from playing with them. Can they think of any toys that adults have? You could think of other shops containing objects that could come to life.

A helping hand

This game focuses on the sense of touch and the children's awareness of everyday objects.

Resources

A selection of everyday objects that are slightly unusual in shape – for example, a garlic crusher, a novelty egg-cup, a fir cone, a retractable tape measure. You will also need a blindfold and a box.

What to do

Ask for a volunteer to wear the blindfold and feel the first object hidden in the box. They then guess what they think it is. Allow a set time for this, so that all the children have a turn. You could play this game over a number of sessions to maintain interest. Ask the children not to call out the identity of an object while a child is trying to guess it.

Comments

You can develop this activity by studying hands more closely. Talk to the children about the qualities of their hands and what they enable them to do. Let the children compare palms to see how different they are.

Rabbit ears

This game promotes observational skills
and concentration.

Resources

None

What to do

Choose a child to be the rabbit. They put up their index fingers
by the side of their head to represent rabbit ears. The child's
neighbours join in by putting up one of their index fingers – the
child on the right puts up one index finger by their left ear, and the
child on the left puts up one index finger by their right ear. Each of
the rabbit's ears is now made of two index fingers.

The rabbit calls the name of another child and all three point the
ears at that child. This child then becomes the new rabbit and the
game is repeated. Each time a new rabbit is chosen the children
need to be concentrating so that they are ready to respond. If the
rabbit's neighbours are not ready to make the ears, the children
close to them can give them a gentle prompt.

Comments

Once the children understand the game, see how fast you can get
the action moving around the circle. Warn the children they must
pay attention, otherwise they may miss a cue.

Body language

This game develops a calm, concentrated mind. The children try to shut out all sensations around them and think carefully about what they are doing.

Resources

Make sure the children have sufficient space to lie down without touching one another.

What to do

Ask the children to lie down, close their eyes and concentrate on what you say. Talk them through various body parts, starting at their feet. For example:

Concentrate on your right foot. Feel the weight of it. Think of each toe. Think of your sole and now your heel. Concentrate on the bones in your ankle. Repeat this with your left foot. Draw an imaginary line from your left foot up to your knee. Think of the shape of your knee. Repeat this with your right leg. Now focus on your pelvis and feel the width of it. Think of your spine. Imagine its strength and flexibility. Sense all the vertebrae. Now feel your shoulders, wide and strong. Think of your right arm from your shoulder to your elbow. Imagine the shape of your elbow and think of it bending and flexing. Imagine your wrist, think how it bends and swivels. Now concentrate on your fingers. Think of how useful and flexible they are. Repeat this for your left arm. Finally, concentrate on your head. Feel how heavy it is. Think about its size and shape. Now lie quietly and enjoy the peace of the moment before I ask you to come back to the circle.

Comments

Make the language and the length of time you spend on this activity suitable for the age of the group. You could ask groups of four or five to think up an exercise programme that focuses on each body part in a different order.

Greetings

In this enjoyable game children use imagination and language skills to greet each other.

Resources

None

What to do

Go round the circle, allowing each child to greet another in the group. They can use their imagination to think of as many different ways as possible. It may be useful to brainstorm some ideas prior to starting the game. The greetings could include shaking hands, a high five, elbow to elbow. The children need to give a verbal greeting using the child's name too, for example:

> *Good morning ...*
> *Hi there ...*
> *Hello ...*

Comments

Make sure that all the children have decided on their chosen form of greeting before you begin. This will avoid wasting time and interrupting the flow of the game. Talk to the children about the importance of greeting people and why it is a ritual. You might even find some interesting greetings used in other countries. This could be something for the children to research.

My object

This game provides an opportunity for children to practise language skills and attention to detail.

Resources

A box containing a selection of items. As this game is about description, look for objects with interesting shapes and textures – such as a pine cone, an unusually shaped leaf, a patterned bead, a shell.

What to do

Invite a child to look at, and feel an object, whilst keeping it concealed in the box. Ask the child to describe their object, without naming it, and let the others guess what it is.

Comments

This game could be played over a number of sessions. It might be a good idea to brainstorm suitable descriptions beforehand so that the children can use these for reference later. You could make an interesting display of the objects, with written descriptions.

Walking a tightrope

This game is an exciting way to explore a range of movements. The children need to imagine a variety of sensations and their physical response to them.

Resources

None. But enough space is needed for the children to move around freely in.

What to do

Tell the children that they are going to mime walking on different surfaces. Ask them to think very carefully about the surface you call out and how they will react to it. Some examples you could use are:

Wet, sticky mud

Hot coals

A tightrope

A noisy marble floor when you are trying to be quiet

Thick sponge

The Moon

A cloud

A river

Tall grass

Comments

You could have more fun with a decree from the Ministry of Silly Walks that everyone must walk in a silly manner. See how inventive the children can be.

Guess what I'm saying

This game explores the use of tone of voice, facial expression and posture in communication.

Resources

A list of sentences (see page 141)

What to do

Divide the children into two groups, A and B. Give each child a sentence from the list for their group and tell them they can only say, 'da – da – da'. Explain that they need to use tone of voice, mime and body language to convey meaning. Ask them to imagine how they would say their sentence before they start. Put the children into pairs, with one child from A and one child from B in each. The children take it in turns to say their nonsense sentence for their partner to guess.

Comments

Tell the children that their guess doesn't have to be exactly right. When it is fairly close the player can give the correct version. If a child is completely stuck, their partner can give a clue. The children can clarify details by asking their partner questions, which are answered using normal language.

This activity is a good starting point for discussing non-verbal language, which is an important factor in how people respond to each other. You can discuss how the children may get better responses from others if they consider the non-verbal content of what they do.

The hat I'm wearing

This game develops children's knowledge and experience of other people in society.

Resources

Some music and five or six different hats – such as a police officer's helmet, a hard hat, a fire-fighter's helmet, a magician's hat, a school cap.

What to do

Decide on one sentence and action to go with each hat. For the police officer's helmet you could say, 'The park is that way' and mime someone giving directions. Try to avoid stereotypical responses. The game begins with the music playing and one hat being passed around the circle. When the music stops, the child left holding the hat says the appropriate sentence and performs the action. The game then continues. More hats can be introduced during the game, depending on the experience of the group.

Comments

This game provides an opportunity to look at why the children will or won't wear certain items of clothing. The children can explore the pressures of needing to belong to, and be accepted by, certain groups.

Snap shots

This game explores how preconceptions influence our judgements about other people.

Resources

A selection of photographs of people cut from magazines. Don't use famous figures that the children know. Instead choose characters whose dress and appearance portray a variety of types; for example, someone young and fashionable, an executive, a farmer, someone who looks rich, someone who looks poor.

What to do

Divide the class into small groups. Give each group two or three photographs. Ask them to study these and discuss what they think the people do and what their backgrounds are, and why they reached these conclusions. Allow 20 minutes for this activity, and then call the groups back to the circle. Ask each group to choose one of their photographs and share their findings.

Comments

Discuss with the children how we all make snap judgements about people based on their appearances. Explore how these can often be wrong, and how getting to know someone can alter our preconceptions.

Product puzzles

This game explores factors that can have an influence on our decision-making.

Resources

A selection of adverts cut from magazines. Try to choose ones that the children will be unfamiliar with. Remove any text that relates to the product, number each image and keep a record of the product. Choose adverts with strong visual clues, such as sportswear, pain relief, beds and cars.

What to do

As a practice round, show the children an advert, talk about the visual clues and ask them to guess the product. The children can then work in small groups, each group having one advert. Ask them to study the advert carefully and decide on the product being advertised. The groups can bring their decisions back to the main circle. Use your checklist to see if they have answered correctly and ask them to explain their reasoning.

Comments

You might like to discuss other questions, such as:

Did similar products use similar advertising?

Were certain adverts aimed at specific ages or community groups?

Can they think of occasions when they bought a product purely because of the influence of an advert?

How susceptible are they to advertising?

The rule of the game

This game develops the skills of observation
and deduction.

Resources

None

What to do

One child leaves the room briefly while the others decide on a rule
for the game, such as they have to put their hand on their right hip
when they answer, or they have to speak in a low voice. Once a rule
is decided the child is invited back in. They ask children questions
that have to be answered according to the rule. They continue until
the rule is guessed. The game is repeated with a different rule and
child.

Comments

It is a good idea to brainstorm ideas for rules before the game
starts, so that the children have an idea of what to look for. Set a
time limit to keep the game moving.

Eyewitness account

This game encourages children to pay attention to detail.
They work together in small groups, each child taking an
equal role to achieve a result.

Resources

A list of events collected on a flipchart, such as: a road accident, the
opening of a new shop, a robbery, a burst water pipe in a restaurant

What to do

Divide the class into groups of four or five. Give each group an event
to prepare. One child in each group is a reporter. The other children
are to pretend they have witnessed the event. Each child must give
an eyewitness account of what they saw. Ask them to concentrate on
the details, such as who was present, how they reacted and what
they said. The reporter interviews the others about the event. After
20 minutes return to the circle and allow each group to perform
their role play.

Comments

You can develop this game by collecting different newspaper articles
about the same story. Ask the children to compare these to see if
there are discrepancies in the details reported. Discuss with the
children why eyewitness reports differ when everyone has seen the
same incident. You could ask the children to study a picture for
several minutes, then question them about it to see what they have
noted.

Six of the best

This is a quick-thinking game that encourages attention to detail and is fun to play.

Resources

Category cards (see page 142) and a 'talking object'

What to do

Ask for a volunteer to begin the game. This child takes a card and tries to say six items that fit the category. Meanwhile everyone else passes the 'talking object' around the circle, trying to complete this before the child finishes their list.

Comments

You can give the child a specific card if you would like greater control over the category each child receives.

Further activities

Wallets and handbags

Ask the children to brainstorm items that might be found in men's wallets and women's handbags. Compare the two lists to see the differences and similarities. Take a vote on the most important item in each.

Paint blobs

Tell the children to make random blobs of paint on some paper. When they have done this, ask them to use felt-tips pens to turn the blobs into animals, either real or imaginary.

Squiggles

Ask the children to close their eyes and draw random squiggles on a piece of paper. When they have finished, ask them to study them and turn them into a picture.

Pen-friend

Tell the children to imagine they have a pen-friend. Ask them to write a letter to them describing themselves, their home, family and hobbies.

Cartoons

Collect a selection of cartoons and block out the text (if any). Ask the children to supply this for the characters, using the cartoon's visual clues to decide what is happening.

Eyewitness

Show the children a short piece of a video and ask them questions about it afterwards. Re-run the excerpt so that they can see how accurate their answers were.

Motivating through music

Music can deepen emotions, raise energy levels and provide inspiration. The games in this section use rhythm and music to energise, release tension, relax, focus concentration and stimulate imagery. A steady, regular rhythm can be used to aid children's movements. Above all, music can be used to create a warm, positive atmosphere, in which self-esteem can flourish.

Rhythmic-cool

This game uses rhythm and tempo to develop concentration skills.

Resources

Simple percussion instruments, such as wood blocks or claves, or short extracts of music with varying tempos, such as:

> 'Fossiles' from *Le Carnaval Des Animaux* by Saint-Saëns
> 'Nimrod' from *Enigma Variations* by Elgar
> Current pop music

What to do

Ask the children to listen carefully to a simple rhythm made by using a percussion instrument or a recording. When it is played a second time they must try to clap in time to it.

Comments

Some children may find this game quite difficult, and you may need to lead the clapping. Ask them to watch very closely and try to keep in time with you. With experience, children can try to establish the tempo independently. You can develop this theme by asking them to lead clapping rhythms unaccompanied. They could also find some clapping rhymes to perform.

Jump to the beat

This game focuses on children's listening skills. It is fun and energising, and requires concentration.

Resources

A tape/CD player and music with a strong, definite beat, such as:

> 'Marche Royale Du Lion' from *Le Carnaval Des Animaux* by Saint-Saëns
> Current pop music
> 'The Arrival of the Queen of Sheba' from *Solomon* by Handel

What to do

Ask the children to listen carefully to a piece of music and move in response to its rhythm. They must try to match their movements to the beat of the music. To begin with you can suggest ways to move; for example, walk, march, skip, hop, jump, tiptoe.

Comments

As they become more experienced you can ask the children to suggest their own ways to move. Discuss with them why they like music, how it makes them feel and why it is so enjoyable.

Orchestral soundtrack

This game encourages children to take an active part
in making music. They will need to listen and
concentrate effectively.

Resources

A selection of percussion instruments – such as tambourines,
triangles, maracas, wood blocks and claves – a recording of familiar
songs and a tape/CD player

What to do

Introduce the instruments and allow the children some time to
explore them. Decide with them on the song they will sing for this
game, plus when and how they will play their instruments. You can
organise this by dividing the children into sections and using hand
movements to conduct them. Rehearse the piece several times until
the children become proficient. You can then record their
performance, play it back and discuss any development points.

Comments

Children will enjoy the opportunity to orchestrate their own song,
which they can do in groups of five or six. They can also make their
own percussion instruments, such as maracas, papier-mâché egg-
shakers and drums. Let them use their imagination, working in pairs
to see what they can design.

Musical dreams

The children are asked to use their imagination to think of scenes suggested by pieces of music. This game is good for relaxation and focusing attention.

Resources

A tape/CD player and music that reflects different moods, such as:

> *An American in Paris* by Gershwin
> *Shepherd Moons* by Enya
> 'Golliwogg's Cake-walk' from *Children's Corner Suite* by Debussy
> 'Troika Song' from *Lieutenant Kije Suite* by Prokofiev

What to do

Ask the children to listen to a piece of music and decide what sort of scene it suggests to them. A lively piece may suggest a circus, fairground or carnival; whilst a quieter scene may suggest a deserted beach or tranquil woodland. Agree on a scene and play the music again, asking the children to sit, relax and close their eyes. Be prepared to talk the children through the scene, telling them the details to imagine.

Comments

Discuss with the children what they imagined as they listened to the music and how easy they found it. How similar or different were their scenes? Explore what the children think it is about music that suggests different scenes.

Voice orchestras

This game is great fun and develops
concentration skills.

Resources

A tape/CD player

What to do

You may want to base this activity on a familiar tune, or have an
idea of how you would like the completed work to sound. Divide the
children into groups of four or five. Give each group a different
sound to make – for example, boom-boom, cha-cha-cha or ting-ting
– and a different pitch to say it in. You will need to use hand
movements to conduct the children as they rehearse their sounds
to produce the familiar tune. It is useful to have actions for start,
stop, louder and softer. Practise with your orchestra until you have
produced a good sound and then record it. The children can listen to
the recording, and then discuss elements they like and those they
would like to improve.

Comments

Children will enjoy producing their own voice orchestras. Ask them
to think up their own sounds. They can be very inventive.

Tricky tempos

This game provides an enjoyable way to develop listening skills. The children need to concentrate in order to keep in time with the tempo.

Resources

None

What to do

Choose one or two simple familiar songs. Tell the children you are going to change the tempo while they are singing and that they must pay careful attention and try to keep in time. It is best to begin this game by singing with the children and using agreed hand movements to indicate a change of tempo. You could use a faster or slower clap, or a metronome, in future games.

Comments

You could use movements, such as marching, in this game too. The children could be invited to volunteer to conduct. Once the children are experienced at changing the tempo, you could introduce other hand movements to control dynamics.

Action songs

This game is an energetic way to develop creative responses to music.

Resources

None

What to do

In groups the children choose a simple familiar song and devise actions, specifically hand movements, to accompany it. Allow the groups 15 minutes to work out their routine, then call them back to the circle and let each group demonstrate their composition.

Comments

If you think the children will have difficulty in thinking of appropriate songs you can brainstorm a list to choose from. You can develop this game by singing familiar action songs, leaving out an additional word each time.

Music and poetry

In this game the children relax to background music and focus on a narrative poem.

Resources

A tape/CD player and some gentle instrumental music, such as:

> *Lark Ascending* by Vaughan Williams
> *Shepherd Moons* by Enya
> 'Le Cygne' from *Le Carnaval Des Animaux* by Saint-Saëns

A suitable narrative poem, for example:

> 'The Walrus and the Carpenter' by Lewis Carroll
> 'Night Mail' by W. H. Auden
> 'The Pied Piper of Hamelin' by Robert Browning
> 'The Mighty Slide' by Allan Ahlberg

What to do

Ask the children to lie down and close their eyes. Play some soft music and ask them to relax, block out all distractions and concentrate on your voice. Read the poem clearly accompanied by the background music.

Comments

Discuss the poem with the children to make sure they understood the story. Ask them how they enjoyed the experience. Older children may like to organise similar sessions in pairs or small groups, choosing their own music and poetry. Ask the children to use gentle music that complements the poem.

Further activities

Ballads

Listen to a song with a storyline; for example, a traditional folk song. Ask the children to discuss how the music contributes to the story.

Music while you work

Play gentle background music while the children are working. Ask them if this helped them to concentrate.

Musical influence

Divide the class into two groups, giving each group the same story title. With adult help, supervise each group in a different room and play them contrasting pieces of music as they discuss their storyline. Compare the story outlines afterwards to see if the music has influenced their thoughts.

Music through the ages

Listen to music from different periods with the children and discuss how music has developed and changed over time. Ask them to comment on any specific differences they noticed between the pieces.

Barn dance

Today children very rarely dance together. Using suitable music, teach them a traditional dance as part of their PE curriculum.

Dance routines

Let the children work out a dance routine to their favourite music as a PE activity.

Taking action

The games in this section provide an opportunity for the group to have fun and let off steam. They can be used to energise, to release tension or as calming exercises. Enjoying such games together is good for the harmony of the group.

Make a move

This game provides energetic movement for the whole group.

Resources

None. You need a large space to move around in.

What to do

Brainstorm a list of things that move in different ways; for example, a dog running, a frog hopping, a tractor driving over muddy ground, a tiger stalking, a giant striding.

Explain to the children that you will call out different things that they must pretend to be as they move.

Comments

You could call out a general movement and ask the children to mime something appropriate; for example, something that moves very slowly, something that takes jumps, something that moves through water, something with wheels.

Wiggle and shake

This energising game provides fun and vigorous movement for a group.

Resources

None

What to do

Starting from their heads and working down to their toes, the children are going to shake and wiggle every part of their bodies. Talk them through head, shoulders, arms, hands, fingers, hips, legs and feet. Ask them to see how many parts they can wiggle and shake at one time.

Comments

You can develop this game by giving children the names of different body parts. They must respond when their part is called out. You can do this singly or in combination; for example, 'Heads shake', 'Fingers wiggle', 'Shoulders, knees and toes wiggle'. Allow a few minutes at the end of the session for the children to calm down. Play the same game, but this time work down the body. As you call out each body part, the children must concentrate on it feeling tired and heavy.

Ice sculptures

This is a useful game for calming down after strenuous exercise or a period of intense concentration.

Resources

None

What to do

Tell the children to pretend they are ice sculptures. Ask them to imagine that they are standing tall and upright. Then the sun comes out. Tell the children to think of it shining down on them as they begin to melt and gradually become smaller until they are just a puddle. Ask the children to mime appropriate movements for this scene.

Comments

If you want to include an activity prior to this exercise, the children can mime carving an ice sculpture in pairs.

Shake your body

Shake your body

This game combines concentration with physical movement.

Resources

None

What to do

Talk the children through a series of movements that start at their heads and end at their toes; for example, head nods, eyes blink, mouth snaps, neck bends, shoulders lift, arms stretch, fingers wiggle, waist turns, hips sway, knees bend, feet hop. Do this sequence twice and then vary the instructions so the children have to listen carefully, such as arms turn, hips bend, shoulders wiggle.

Comments

Line the children up and send a movement along the line to create a ripple effect. Repeat this game in a circle, introducing commands to change the direction of the movement.

Clap and call

This exciting game develops concentration skills and is great fun.

Resources

Sticky labels (one for each child)

What to do

Number the children around the circle, giving each one a sticky label with a number on it. A child begins the game by saying their number and somebody else's. The second child repeats the process, saying their own and a third number. All the children clap twice in-between the pairs of numbers.

Comments

If you start the game standing, children can sit down after they have had a turn to ensure everyone has a go.

All change

All change

This game is fun for children to play, but requires concentration.

Resources

None

What to do

The children stand in a circle. One child begins by performing an action, such as clap twice or patting knees once. The other children join in until you tap a different child on the shoulder. This child then starts a new action. The children must concentrate to notice and copy any new actions.

Comments

It may be a good idea to discuss suitable actions with the children beforehand to avoid any hesitation later. A variation would be to pass the action on from child to child around the circle, rather than in unison. You could then start two actions in different places for some real excitement.

Queue for action

This game provides whole group involvement that
is good fun.

Resources

None

What to do

Ask the children to stand in a line with their backs to you. Tell them
they can turn round only when someone touches them on the
shoulder. Tap the first child on the shoulder and when they turn
round perform an action and say, 'Pass it on.' The action continues
along the line until it reaches the last child. This child performs the
action to compare it with the original action.

Comments

The children will enjoy seeing how fast they can pass the action
along the line. Use a stopwatch to time them and set a record. The
children can take turns at initiating the action at the start of the
line.

Action orchestra

This game can energise or calm the children, depending on what is needed.

Resources

None. You need plenty of space to move around in.

What to do

Divide the children into groups of four. Give each group a different action to perform, such as running on the spot or bunny jumps. Discuss the hand movements you will use to direct the children. You will need different signals for group in, group out, slower, faster, all together and stop. Conduct the groups in an action orchestra, changing the group involvement and speed of action.

Comments

When the children are more experienced, they can choose their own actions and take turns at conducting.

Altered images

This is a fast and furious action game for the whole group to enjoy.

Resources

None

What to do

The children stand in a large circle, leaving spaces between each other. Explain to them that they are going to pretend to be wizards who can change other people's shape. The game starts with two wizards, one in the form of a cat and the other of a mouse. The cat chases the mouse in and out of the gaps between the children. At any point the child being chased can tap another child on the shoulder, change them into an animal that would scare the chaser and take their place in the circle. For example, a dog could chase a cat. The wizard says, 'I change you into …'

Explain to the children that their chosen animal need not be bigger; it could be a mouse chasing an elephant. Whilst the changeover is taking place the chasing must stop.

Comments

It might be a good idea to talk through possible changes before playing this game for the first time. Once the children have got the idea they will be able to think of their own image changes. Encourage children to be inventive in their choices; for example, changing into fire, ice or darkness. If a child suggests an image that is challenged, either decide yourself who is the chaser or ask the children to vote on whether to accept it or not.

All change in the circle

All change in the circle

This is an energetic and enjoyable game that develops concentration skills.

Resources

None

What to do

The children stand in a large circle. Ask them to move around the circle in different ways; for example, skipping, hopping, crawling, walking sideways, walking backwards slowly, galloping, using bunny hops. The children need to be alert to hear the changes called and to avoid any pile-ups.

Comments

You may like to introduce a change direction instruction in later games. Try to finish with a fairly sedate last round to calm the children down. Ask the children to volunteer new ways of moving to see how inventive they can be. With experience some children may like to be the caller.

Ball bearings

This game is useful for developing drama skills and for focusing the children's attention on what they are doing.

Resources

None

What to do

Explain to the children that they are going to mime activities using a ball. They must pay particular attention to the timing of their actions to make the mime realistic. Begin by asking them to pretend to bounce their ball. You can continue this with other actions, such as throw and catch, bowl, shoot at a net, kick, dribble, throw and kick. Ask the children to find a partner and mime throwing the ball backwards and forwards between them.

Comments

Divide the class into groups and ask them to work out a mime together for a ball game; for example, rounders or netball. For this game the children will need to consider fielding, bowling, batting and running. After 15 minutes the groups can return to the circle and perform their mimes to the others.

Rocket launch

This game combines action with developing concentration skills and is great fun to play.

Resources

None

What to do

Count how many people, including yourself, are in the room. That number starts your countdown. Sitting in a circle, children count down from the starting number. Anybody can stand up and call the next number, but if *two* children stand up at the same time, the countdown has to begin again. When you reach 1, all the children stand, raise their arms and shout, 'We have lift-off.'

Comments

Warn the children to be vigilant and to avoid standing at the same time as someone else. Once the children have grasped the idea of the game, get them to see how quickly they can call out the numbers.

Musical islands

This game encourages cooperation and imagination.

Resources

A tape/CD player and some music, small mats or non-slip markers

What to do

Spread the mats out on the floor as the islands. Tell the children that while the music is playing they must move about in the sea. When the music stops they must find an island to stand on or they will be out. Explain to the children that you will gradually remove the islands and that they will need to cooperate so that as many children as possible can squeeze on them. Any child with a foot in the sea will be deemed out and can join in after the next round.

Comments

You can end the session by playing a conventional game of musical islands, with only one child per island until you have a winner.

Further activities

Three-legged mime

Tell the children they are going to mime being in a three-legged race. They must practise moving with a partner. Ask them to see how quickly they can move, keeping in time.

Ball around the circle

Develop ball skills with younger children by rolling, bouncing or throwing the ball to each child around the circle.

Team ball games

Get each team to line up and pass the ball alternately over their heads or between their legs. When the ball reaches the front that child runs to the back of the line and starts the pattern again. The game ends when the child who started returns to the front.

Planning activity

Divide the class into groups and let each group plan an activity they would like to do. You will need to discuss their plans with them to make sure they are workable before putting them into practice.

Moving in different ways

Ask the children to think of as many ways as possible to move on their feet, hands and feet or in pairs.

Activities for healthy living

Talk to the children about the need for physical activity in their lives. Ask them what happens if people don't take any physical exercise. Talk to them about the various forms of physical activity they take, or could take, outside school.

Photocopiable materials

Matching pairs and Yes or no

cat

book

cap

house

cup

hen

dog

tree

sock

fish

flower

pencil

teddy

shoe

hat

car

spoon

chair

Scrambled stories

Scrambled stories

Yes or no

Bicycle	Scooter	Tree
Swimming pool	Dog	Cake
Boat	Frog	Ambulance
Mountain	Swing	Newspaper
Parachute	Fire engine	Flower
Football	Kettle	Train
Spoon	Tractor	Pen
Necklace	Computer	Sandwich
Hat	Television	Plate
Mobile phone	Lorry	Aeroplane
Apple	Shoe	Purse
Car	Ruler	Watch

A picture paints a thousand words

Submarine Elephant Waterfall	Volcano Tent Polar bear	Mountain Giant Carriage
Palace Diamond Tiger	Genie Cloak Boat	Cake Train Umbrella
Skunk Jungle Basket	Top hat Gold Carpet	Spider Banana Picnic
Museum Parrot Bracelet	Slipper Motorbike Valley	Avalanche Kangaroo Mud
Star Banquet Snake	Crown Ostrich Cloak	Oak tree Superhero Whale
Dragon Ice Rocket	Lake Dungeon Cave	Firework Island Gorilla

Happy families

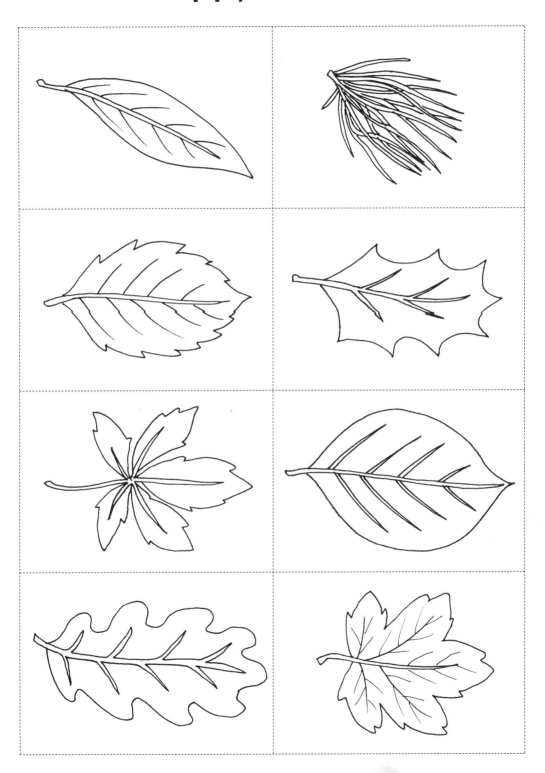

Back to the start (1)

You have fallen over in the park and cut your knee.	You are at a concert to see a famous pop singer.
You want to buy a new CD in a shop.	You have spilt water over a really good picture you have just painted.
You have forgotten to do your homework.	A crab has nipped your big toe on a beach.
You are about to make a parachute jump.	You are stuck in a lift that has broken down.
The chip pan has caught fire at home.	Your big toe has got stuck in the bath tap.
You are putting up a tent.	Your bicycle has a flat tyre.
You have locked yourself out of your house.	Your pet hamster has escaped.
Your dog has fleas.	You are in an earthquake.
A car has run into the back of your car.	Your cat is stuck up a tree.

Back to the start (2)

You are walking with your laces tied together.	Your train is an hour late.
You have taken your injured cat to the vet.	You have just had an injection.
You have just had a tooth pulled out.	You have a splinter in your foot.
You have dropped your dinner on the floor.	A bat has flown into your room.
A baby is crying for its dummy.	You have scored the winning goal in the cup final.
You are building a sandcastle.	You are using a skipping rope.
You have just heard a funny joke.	You are riding a horse.
You are feeding fish to a killer whale.	You are flying a kite.
You are diving off a diving board.	You are taking an energetic dog for a walk.

You choose (1)

1 What would you prefer to do?

a) Read a book ☐ b) Go for a swim ☐

c) Watch TV ☐ d) Visit a friend. ☐

2 Which animal do you like best?

a) Elephant ☐ b) Tiger ☐

c) Whale ☐ d) Chimpanzee. ☐

3 What would make you most angry?

a) Being let down by a friend ☐ b) Losing your pocket money ☐

c) Not being able to visit a friend ☐ d) Forgetting your homework. ☐

4 Which would you find most frightening?

a) A volcano erupting ☐ b) An earthquake ☐

c) An avalanche ☐ d) A tornado. ☐

5 Which do think is most important?

a) Being rich ☐ b) Being healthy ☐

c) Being popular ☐ d) Being intelligent. ☐

6 Which would you most like to do?

a) Parachute jumping ☐ b) Deep-sea diving ☐

c) Mountain climbing ☐ d) Driving a racing car. ☐

7 Which would you rather eat?

a) Snails ☐ b) Squid ☐

c) Sheep's eyes ☐ d) Ants. ☐

8 What would you rather be?

a) Dolphin ☐ b) Tiger ☐

c) Otter ☐ d) Eagle. ☐

9 What kind of holiday would you prefer?

a) Sun and sea ☐ b) Sporting ☐

c) Safari ☐ d) Skiing. ☐

You choose (2)

10 Which meal do you prefer?

  a) Fish and chips ☐   b) Spaghetti bolognaise ☐
  c) Chicken curry ☐   d) Pizza. ☐

11 What sort of book do you like?

  a) Thriller ☐   b) Comedy ☐
  c) Fantasy ☐   d) Sports story. ☐

12 How would you rather travel?

  a) By boat ☐   b) By plane ☐
  c) By train ☐   d) By coach. ☐

13 Which pet would you rather have?

  a) Dog ☐   b) Cat ☐
  c) Pony ☐   d) Snake. ☐

14 Which colour do you prefer?

  a) Red ☐   b) Blue ☐
  c) Green ☐   d) Yellow. ☐

15 How would you prefer to spend an evening?

  a) Going to a party ☐   b) Going to the cinema ☐
  c) Staying at home ☐   d) Going to a swimming pool. ☐

16 Which would you prefer to do?

  a) Cycling ☐   b) Swimming ☐
  c) Skateboarding ☐   d) Walking. ☐

17 Which city would you prefer to visit?

  a) Rome ☐   b) Paris ☐
  c) Delhi ☐   d) London. ☐

18 Which do you think is the scariest?

  a) A spider ☐   b) Brussels sprouts ☐
  c) A noise in the night ☐   d) Half a maggot in the apple
                               you have just bitten into. ☐

Plus points

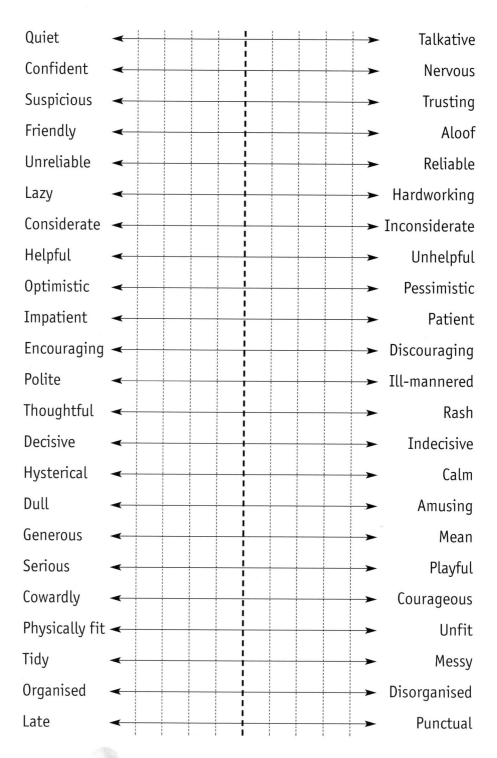

Quiet	←——————————→	Talkative
Confident	←——————————→	Nervous
Suspicious	←——————————→	Trusting
Friendly	←——————————→	Aloof
Unreliable	←——————————→	Reliable
Lazy	←——————————→	Hardworking
Considerate	←——————————→	Inconsiderate
Helpful	←——————————→	Unhelpful
Optimistic	←——————————→	Pessimistic
Impatient	←——————————→	Patient
Encouraging	←——————————→	Discouraging
Polite	←——————————→	Ill-mannered
Thoughtful	←——————————→	Rash
Decisive	←——————————→	Indecisive
Hysterical	←——————————→	Calm
Dull	←——————————→	Amusing
Generous	←——————————→	Mean
Serious	←——————————→	Playful
Cowardly	←——————————→	Courageous
Physically fit	←——————————→	Unfit
Tidy	←——————————→	Messy
Organised	←——————————→	Disorganised
Late	←——————————→	Punctual

Guess what I am

Spade	Bottle	Bus
Telephone	Television	Kettle
Photograph	Armchair	Washing-up liquid
Spoon	Pillow	Helicopter
Table	Chair	Basketball
Apple	Bin	Mug
Saucepan	Fork	Computer
Carpet	Vase	Egg
Mop	Clock	Glove
Teapot	Curtain	Book
Bed	Microwave	Scissors
Pencil	Paperclip	Telephone

The truth will out (1)

Accomplice – partner in crime (*true*)	Accomplice – type of policeman
Accomplice – small insect	Caber – tree trunk tossed in Scottish sport (*true*)
Caber – taxi driver	Caber – tropical fish
Edelweiss – alpine flower (*true*)	Edelweiss – mountaineering helmet
Edelweiss – gardening tool	Gondola – boat used in Venice (*true*)
Gondola – type of cheese	Gondola – Spanish bullfighter
Incantation – words used for a magic spell (*true*)	Incantation – canning machine
Incantation – savoury dish	Majority – greater number (*true*)
Majority – army officer	Majority – Australian crow

The truth will out (2)

Bibliophile – book lover (*true*)	Bibliophile – cupboard for storing babies' bibs
Bibliophile – glass bottle	Dinghy – small boat (*true*)
Dinghy – dull place	Dinghy – wild dog
Farthingale – hooped petticoat (*true*)	Farthingale – old-fashioned coin
Farthingale – a type of wind	Haggis – Scottish meat dish (*true*)
Haggis – old woman	Haggis – type of beard
Lemming – small rodent (*true*)	Lemming – evergreen tree
Lemming – undersized lamb	Culver – dove or pigeon (*true*)
Culver – type of flower	Culver – dark corner

In the driving seat

Motorbike saddle	Bus seat
Dentist's chair	Seat in a horse-drawn cart
Seat in a speedboat	Seat on the London Eye
Seat in a racing car	Seat on a roller coaster
Seat on a lawnmower	Seat on a crane
Saddle on a racehorse	Saddle on a camel
Seat in a pedal car	Wheelchair
Train seat	A deck chair
Cashier's seat	Piano stool
Seat on a roundabout	A swing

Guess what I'm saying

'Look out, there's a wasp!'
Use voice and expression to show danger.

'Don't draw on my book.'
This is an angry command.

'I've just seen a ghost.'
Try to sound absolutely terrified.

'Please let me go to the disco.'
Use a pleading tone of voice.

'I've fallen out with my best friend.'
Try to sound miserable and lonely.

'I hate vegetables.'
Use a displeased tone of voice.

'Help, the house is on fire!'
You need to show panic and terror.

'What a lovely dog.'
Let your voice and face show admiration.

'It's my birthday today!'
Show excitement in the way you say this.

'How much farther to walk?'
Try to sound tired and fed up.

'For goodness sake, hurry up!'
You need to sound impatient.

'Where are my trainers?'
Try to sound puzzled.

Six of the best

Towns	Fruit	Trees
Farm animals	Dogs	Films
Countries	Books	Capital cities
Items of clothing	Makes of car	Pets
Football teams	Famous buildings	Birds
Musical instruments	Breakfast cereals	Tools
Sports	Family members	Pop stars
Colours	Film stars	Drinks
Television programmes	Items of furniture	Flowers
Historical figures	Fish	Weather conditions
Chocolate bars	Vegetables	Mammals
Team games	Children's authors	Cartoon characters

Training and resources

Jenny Mosley INSET courses

The following courses and workshops are available from a team of highly qualified and experienced consultants, who can be contacted through:

Jenny Mosley Consultancies
8 Westbourne Road
Trowbridge
Wiltshire   Tel: 01225 767157
BA14 0AJ   Fax: 01225 755631

Email: circletime@jennymosley.demon.co.uk
Web site: www.circle-time.co.uk

Promoting happier lunchtimes
Turn your school round – an introduction
A whole school approach to building self-esteem through Circle Time
Assessing the effectiveness of your self-esteem, anti-bullying and positive behaviour policies
Raising staff morale through team-building
Practical activities to maintain and develop the power of Circle Time
A workshop of games to enrich class and lunchtimes

Training support for your workplace

The Jenny Mosley Consultancies' well-trained personnel, experienced in all aspects of the Quality Circle Time model, are available to visit your workplace to give courses and workshops to all your teaching and support staff.

We run both closure and in-school days. In the closure day, all staff, teachers, teaching assistants, lunchtime supervisors and administration staff are invited to team-building and developing moral values through Golden Rules, Incentives and Sanctions, and Ideas for Happier Lunchtimes.

During the in-school day the school does not close and the Quality Circle Time method is demonstrated with whole classes of children, observed by a range of staff. In addition to this, Circle Time meetings are held for lunchtime supervisors and an Action Plan for the school is considered with key members of staff.

Training the trainer courses

Key people may be trained either to go back to their school or their LEA as accredited trainers, responsible for supporting all adults and children in their community through the Jenny Mosley model. For details of ongoing courses contact Jenny Mosley Consultancies on 01225 767157 or via their web site or email.

Quality Circle Time training manuals and resources

Mosley, J. and Thorp, G. (2002) All Year Round, LDA
Mosley, J. and Thorp, G. (2002) Playground Games, LDA
Mosley, J. and Thorp, G. (2002) Lunchtime Notelets, LDA
Mosley, J. and Sonnet, H. (2002) Making Waves – Parachute Games, LDA
Mosley, J. (1993) Turn Your School Round, LDA
Mosley, J. (1997) Quality Circle Time, LDA
Mosley, J. (1998) More Quality Circle Time, LDA
Mosley, J. (1996) Golden Rules posters, LDA
Mosley, J. (1996) Class reward sheets, LDA
Mosley, J. (1996) Reward certificates, LDA
Mosley, J. (1996) Responsibility badges, LDA
Mosley, J. (1996) Stickers, LDA
Mosley, J. (2000) Quality Circle Time kit, LDA
Mosley, J. (2000) Quality Circle Time in Action, LDA
Goldthorpe, M. and Nutt, L. (2000) Assemblies to teach Golden
        Rules, LDA
Goldthorpe, M. (1998) Poems for Circle Time and Literacy Hour, LDA
Goldthorpe, M. (1998) Effective IEPs through Circle Time, LDA

For a full range of Jenny Mosley's books and resources please ring LDA customer services on 01945 463441.

Radbrook LRC